The PURSUIT of LOVE

A Woman's Discovery of The Power of Forgiveness

Yvette M. Jones

Copyright © 2000 by Yvette M. Jones

All rights reserved. No part of this publication may be reproduced, stored in any retrievable system, or transmitted in any form, copying, recording or otherwise, without prior permission of the author.

Edited by Dr. Dennis Hensley
Cover design by Carolyn Utesch

ISBN 09705375-0-8

The PURSUIT of LOVE

A story that encourages you, the reader to find freedom through forgiveness

Contents

Dedication 7
Foreword 9
Introduction 10

Chapter 1   Fear of The Giants 13
Chapter 2   The Valley of The Shadow of Death 20
Chapter 3   The Dungeon of Darkness 27
Chapter 4   The Land of Canaan 36
Chapter 5   A Winning Attitude 45
Chapter 6   Why Forgive? 54

About the Author 60
Resources 62

Dedication

To my husband, Dr. Joseph Jones, Ph.D., whose gentleness and unconditional love led the way down the road to healing of damaged emotions.

To my two daughters, whose presence and love has been the healing balm in my life.

To my Lord and Savior, Jesus Christ whose everlasting love broke the chain, delivered me from the house of bondage, healed me and gave me freedom to forgive.

To all of you who encouraged me through your prayers, endorsements and exhortations. My heart is overflowing with joy because you believed that I could write and publish my story. Thank you!

To all the readers, may the Lord Jesus Christ free you to love again and to become fully persuaded that God is able to complete the work He has begun in you.

Foreward

To look at Yvette Jones today, you'd think she had been born with a silver spoon in her mouth. Her photo has graced the cover of *Clarity Magazine*, she has been the focus of major feature articles in such periodicals as *Purpose Magazine* and *Excellence Christian Woman's Magazine*, she is in demand as a speaker nationwide at women's conferences, she is an administrator at a highly esteemed 150-year old private college, and she runs her own private business in custom-made dolls. What a success story, right? Then add to all that the fact that she is pretty, vivacious, and a wonderful wife to her husband Dr. Joseph Jones and a great mom to two lovely daughters. Why, this woman has it all. Some gals just get all the breaks.

The surprise to all this, as you are about to read in this fascinating life story of *The Pursuit of Love*, is that Yvette Jones today should be at the bottom of society's heap. By all accounts, she should be the greatest failure mankind has ever known. In truth, she had nothing going for her when she was young—a broken home, poverty, poor schooling, racial hatred, abandonment, sexual discrimination. However, by the grace of God and through the strong faith and love of the man who became her husband, Yvette rose from a nothing life to an everything life.

Yvette's story will make you cry, but it will also show you what determination and faith can do. Here is a woman who is a role model for people of all generations. Read her story and share in her ministry of healing for all. She is an amazing woman, and her life makes for an amazing book.

Dr. Dennis E. Hensley
author of *Making The Most of Your Potential*

Introduction

Writing this book feels more like a surprising adventure of white water rafting than a predictable "next effort" in reaching my destiny.

However, what I am now writing reflects the thoughts that have been hanging around in the corners of my mind for a long time, thinking that has recently dominated center stage. After twenty years of motivating thousands of people at seminars, retreats, churches across America, colleges and universities, and fund raising events, I wonder how one woman could help in the healing process of so many hurting people. I have been consumed by the desire to write this book in the hope that it will be a motivational tool to encourage many to believe that God is able to heal damaged emotions.

The major thrust that propelled me to "Do It Now" was the multiple requests I received from women and teenagers for a book about my life's journey. Many asked that I write a book explaining the journey that brought me to where I could forgive those who had abused and abandoned me. The desire to help others make the choice to forgive and to gain insight to the truth that forgiveness is possible has been my inspiration to write my story.

My journey began on Fear Alley in New York, the place where I was violated as a child. Sexual abuse damaged my self worth to the point that I became suicidal. After numerous suicide attempts, I became enchanted with the idea of death. Everything around me seemed to support the idea that premature death would be the best way to cope. The desire to die created for me a *Valley of the Shadow of Death*. The *Valley of the Shadow of Death* was the place where love, joy, peace, and hope became strangers in the dark cloud of death. Thoughts of dying took center stage in my mind. Those who had suffered similar afflictions were the travelers of the *Valley of the Shadow of Death*, people whose families had cast them out as worthless individuals. In the Valley of the Shadow of Death, the residents were those who hated self and life. They moved to the Valley to find self-assisted, afflicted death to quickly escape the pain and torments of abuse and abandonment.

Through this book you, the reader, will travel to various areas of my life. You will face the *Fear of the Giants*, the aftermath of sexual abuse, walk toward the Valley of the Shadow of Death, and enter the *Dungeon of Darkness*. It is my intention that these wilderness experiences will paint the scenic backdrops of my life. You will get a picture of the pain of my childhood, and why I chose forgive. On this journey I will share the insights I have gained from biblical teachings regarding the freedom and growth that comes to those who choose to forgive. This book by no means will suggest that forgiveness and healing of damaged emotions is quick and easy, nor that it offers any magical formula. It is intended solely to communicate the message that reaching forgiveness and healing is not a mission impossible. It will cost you pain and sacrifice, but Christ has already paid the price that enables you freely to give forgiveness. Although my story stopped at *Why Forgive*, it is a continuous journey that will end on the Streets of Gold when I leave this earth for the city whose builder is God.

My prayer is that as you begin this journey with me, your *Pursuit of Love* will end at the cross of Jesus Christ, the source of true love. It is the truth about forgiveness that breaks the yokes, frees the captives, and heals the broken and wounded heart. May God's truth enable you to make the right choice and choose the journey leading to forgiveness that will, no doubt, set you free.

*The land...is a land
that eateth up the inhabitants...
all the people that we
saw in it are men of great
stature. There we saw the giants*

Numbers 13:32-33 (KJV)

CHAPTER ONE

Fear of the Giants

Although sexual abuse is a subject that most rape victims would rather hide and keep secret because of the emotional pain involved, I have elected to share my story in print form. It is my desire to have a positive effect on the lives of all who read this story and to encourage the abused and abandoned, proving that it is possible to be healed from damaged emotions.

My emotional response in dealing with the haunting memories of being sexually abused as a child has given me an understanding of the pain experienced by those with similar experiences. I have learned how guilt, fear, lack of self-worth, and depression have long term effects that prevent an individual from maturing emotionally and spiritually.

My story begins with *Fear of the Giants*. This was my perspective of the size or stature of those who sexually abused me. I was five years old when a stranger abducted me from school. The police found me late that night lying in blood on a rooftop in New York City. After being rushed to the emergency room, I was under intense questioning by the police as to who attacked me. However, I had lost all memory of the attacker's physical description. The thought of how I was being sewed up like a turkey consumed my mind. During the 50's, the Thanksgiving turkey was stuffed with bread stuffing and sewed with a black thread. I viewed this scene as I looked between my legs as I received thirty-nine stitches in my vaginal area. It was at this time that I was diagnosed as being sterile, never able to conceive children.

We lived in Harlem, New York in a two room (not two bedrooms) apartment on Park Avenue. One of those rooms was the living room that became the bedroom at night. We had a sleep sofa that all three children slept on. When it was bedtime, I cried because of the pain from the stitches. I had to share the bed with my six-year-old sister and seven-year-old brother.

I felt rejected and began to blame myself for what happened because my mother's attitude toward me was different. Whenever I tried to talk about what had happened, she seemed angry with me. I began to believe that she hated the sight of me. To protect myself from any further pain of rejection, I refused to share my feelings with anyone because of my fear of being rejected. I pretended that the attack never happened; but, inwardly, I felt that I was a bad girl. I accepted the blame that the rape was my fault, and I began to hate myself. I was confused as to why I was to blame for what someone had done to hurt me and why no one seemed to care about my feelings.

David Finkelhor suggests that many victims of sexual abuse experience large amounts of guilt related to his/her abuse. The negative reactions from others and the blaming of the victim for the abuse creates guilt (Finkelhor, p. 190). According to Bierker it is common for survivors of sexual abuse to experience self-blame and a feeling of being responsible for the abuse. The response to guilt is usually in the form of self-punishment, because the victim thinks he/she is bad (Bierker, p.93).

By the time I turned twelve, I had experienced many forms of molestation, child brutality, abuse and abandonment in a dysfunctional family that was filled with violence. Years of violation had left me without self-worth. One devastating night, the remainder of my self-image was shattered. It was the night my mother was out-of-town, in Washington, DC, when my stepfather made me the target of his sexual pleasures. I tried to defend my little body from his attack but his death threats had a weakening effect on me. I slowly stopped fighting back. When I called my mother to report the incident, she refused to believe me. Afterward I became afraid of everyone; even the movements of my mother caused me to jump.

The more I feared being raped again, the more abusers became like giants who were too big for a grasshopper size girl to overcome. Their stature was frightening and their voices terrified me into surrendering to their lustful desires. This caused me to build up a defense shield of self-condemnation and self-hatred. I pretended that it no longer mattered what happened to me.

One abuser came to my mother's home weekly to cash in on sexual favors, as he chose to hypnotize me with a little circular disc with moving lines. I could hear his voice telling me, "Your eyes are getting heavy with sleep. Now, sleep, sleep. When you wake up you will not remember a thing." But I remembered everything. I felt like vomiting when he touched me and played with the private parts of my body. I hated every moment of it and wanted to cry for help, but there was no one to help. Although my mother was in the next room, I would not tell her what this child molester was doing in her house for fear she would deny the truth. If my mother had chosen to believe me, she could risk losing child support from the father of one of my siblings.

In the midst of the sexual abuse, I was also facing child abuse in the form of verbal and physical attacks. Harsh words continued to eat away any remaining fragment of self-worth, filling me with hatred and anger. I remember being called a "tramp" and "stupid." The words, "The older you get, the dumber you get," and "I am going to send you to 'live' with your father" continuously tormented me. By the age of 10, I had only seen my biological father twice, once being at his funeral. I had no remembrance of living with him. It appeared he impregnated my mother with three children, but never supported us. To be threatened to live with someone I had only heard violent reports about increased my fear.

From the age of five until I was 35, I feared being the target of those addicted to unsolicited and forceful sexual activities. On my honeymoon I realized that the fear of rape was a spiritual battle that could only be won through trusting in Jesus Christ. Every night of my honeymoon I was terrified by nightmares of running down a dark alley from a perpetrator. In the dreams I was so terrified of being raped, I would wake up screaming. The silent filled nights only set the stage for the devil to use fear to take overcome me with the torments of the past. I remember waking up sensing the presence of evil in the room, as if I was being dared to return to sleep.

My initial reaction to the nightmares was fear. When I tried to keep alert and awake, a heavy cloud of sleep crept in like a thief in the night and overtook me. We had to shorten our honeymoon because the quietness of Cape Cod was so overwhelming it intensified my fears.

The emotional impact of sexual abuse has caused many victims to experience similar fears that engrave a permanent image of the attack in the memory bank. The fear of being alone, of being harmed, and of crowds has paralyzed the emotional and psychological development of many victims. Dreams and nightmares of sexual assault and crying out during sleep have been the long-term effects on those who were victims during their childhood (Geiscr, p. 26-27).

Throughout the scriptures, the words "Fear Not" appear to encourage those bound by terrorizing fear. The apostle Paul says, "God did not give us the spirit of fear...."(II Timothy 1:7). In Romans 8:15 it is written, "For you did not receive a spirit that makes you a slave again to fear, but you received the Spirit of sonship (or daughtership)." These scriptures suggest that it is not God's will for his sons and daughters to be tormented and imprisoned by fear. It has been reported that 90% of chronic patients visit physicians because of the common symptom of fear. According to the following story, fear kills:

In his sermon on fear, Clarence E. Macartney describes a peasant, driving into a European city, who was hailed by an aged woman. As they drove along, the peasant became alarmed as he learned his passenger was the plague, Cholera. But she assured him that only ten people in the city would die of Cholera. She even offered the peasant a dagger, saying he could slay her if more than ten died. But more than a hundred perished. As the angry peasant drew the dagger to deal a death blow, the plague lifted her hand and protested, "Wait! I killed only ten. Fear killed the rest!" (Tan, p. 439)

As in the above illustration, fear became cancerous within me as it set up colonies that slowly ate away any form of peace. I had no sense of security and felt unprotected. I was angry with my mother and blamed her for my emotional pain. This anger was internalized and manifested itself by inflicted pain on myself. Someone had to pay for the bitterness and anger that raged out of control within me. The attitude of self-condemnation and self-hatred began to usher me into the next phase of my journey. Onward to the *Valley of the Shadow of Death*, the place where suicide became a way to escape the earth below. The *Valley of the Shadow of Death* offered me a way out of coping with life. Not knowing the darkness that was straight ahead, I would soon embark on the darkest season of my life. My journey through the *Valley of the Shadow of Death* took a temporary detour after an attempt at suicide, when I was committed to the custody of the state of New York. In essence, I became a foster child of the state, separated from all family ties. My already damaged emotions suffered an additional blow when I realized that I was alone in a world filled with people, and absent of love. No child is strong enough to handle such a hard lesson that no one wants to love him or her.

The words to "You've Lost That Loving Feeling" were the last words I heard after I took pills to end my life. The words of the Righteous Brothers song echoed in my mind as I thought on my experiences in which love had been a foreigner whose language I had not learned.

Awaking to life and disappointment became a dark cloud experience. Death had rejected me. I was lost for ideas on how to end an unwanted life. I should have died from the large dosage of pills; instead, I was given a second chance. I did not want a second chance to live life without love. This created a gross darkness over my vision of life which turned into depression and an

"I don't care what happens to me attitude." I decided to give up on death and life by surrendering my mind to the darkness of hopelessness. Depression began to fill my days with despair over the defeat with suicide. I began to believe that I was a complete failure. Even death lost its sting and would not accept my invitation.

The desire to reunite with my family had died. When told that my release day from Bellevue Hospital was approaching, I threatened to attempt suicide again if I was sent back home. The option to spend my teen years at the *Dungeon of Darkness*, better known as the state asylum, became a welcomed choice. I willingly accepted the only alternative left for a fatherless child who felt trapped in the darkest mental dungeon of hopelessness. I literally did not care what the future had in store, or what was down the road at the *Dungeon of Darkness*. The state hospital was going to be my home away from home. I had no choice but to accept my new home and crazy family. At least they knew they had a problem and accepted the diagnosis to receive psychiatric treatment.

*Even though I walk
through the
Valley of The Shadow of Death
I will fear no evil*

Psalm 23:4 (NIV)

CHAPTER TWO

The Valley of the Shadow of Death

My emotional response in dealing with death and dying has given me an understanding of the grief process. I have lost several loved ones who were influential in my life. Experiences with grief of lose have taught me how denial, anger, and suicidal tendency, can hinder spiritual and physical maturity and develop into an unforgiving spirit.

When I was born, my mother was only sixteen years old. I was the third child born to this teenage mother. The two children born before me were eleven months apart in age. During this time, my mother had chosen not to give me up for adoption but to have me live with her aunt. I lived with this aunt off and on for several years, with periodic visits to New York to see my mother. On one visit in 1959, I did not know that I would never see my Aunt Dora again. She dropped me off with the idea that she would return for me one day. I waited for her return, but she never came back for me.

While I was playing outside, I was asked by a relative, "Do you know where everyone has gone?" I replied, "No." I was told that the family had gone to Aunt Dora's funeral. I stood in silence. I do not remember crying. Finding out that Aunt Dora died and no one had taken me to the funeral constructed a steel wall in my heart, and bitterness, resentment, and hatred were the construction crew. I refused, after that, to let anyone get close enough to hurt me again. Although I chose to keep my tears within, I was deeply hurt that such important information had been withheld. Aunt Dora had been special to me and no one cared or understood about how much I loved her.

I remember the special moments I had spent with her, kneeling at the window of her house and looking into the black star filled sky. She taught me how to prayer. She introduced me to cheesecake and was responsible for me being a lover of cheesecake.

The sad part about the impact of Aunt Dora's death is that, even today, I have no image in my memory of what she looked like. I long to see an image of this angel in my life, but there's nothing. I have a complete mental block regarding her physical characteristics. Only the Creator knows who this lady was who became my mother for a season of my developmental years. She never claimed to be my mother, but made sure I visited my mother occasionally. It appears we lived in Florida and North Carolina. Some of my relatives confirm this idea, but no one has given me any addresses or names. Areas of my life remain in the dark of the unknown.

The experience of being excluded from Aunt Dora's funeral was unforgivable. My heart was filled with a spirit of bitterness and hatred toward my mother. I blamed her because she knew how close I was to her aunt. I was determined never to forgive my mother.

The impact of this death pushed me more into becoming an introvert and loner. I refused to talk much, and smiling was a lost art. I remember a teacher saying that I had only spoken a few words the whole school year. I became extremely quiet and kept to myself. I felt that I did not fit into the "In Crowd," as it was termed in those days. I was poor in material wealth and family love. I never knew my father, and sometimes there was not enough food to go around to feed all of us. I remember standing in food lines for American cheese loafs, powered milk, oat meal, and green beans that had black letters on the label. The writing on the label confirmed that we were poor because it read "Not To Be Sold." I thought, "this stuff is so bad that it can't be sold. So feed it to the poor, they won't know the difference."

I continued to keep my feelings and thoughts private as I entertained the idea of suicide to escape the poverty-stricken life, a life destitute of love and provisions. When thoughts of losing the only friend I knew would flood my mind, I would repress my feelings to the point of numbness. I pretended that I was someone else that this had not happened to me. My mind separated me from the grief I felt in losing someone dear to me. I had no one to turn to who understood or would much less listen to a kid. I felt completely lost and alone. I thought, "Here I am among a bunch of strangers who were my family." No one seemed to have time for love.

To react in shock and denial is to repress feelings and refuse to accept death. Children often respond to grief by overcompensating for their feelings through making believe that the crisis never occurred (Davidson, 1990). Adults cope with death through denying the loss after saying, "This can't be true."

No matter what the underlying reasons are for emotional reactions toward death and dying, everyone needs to find the appropriate method to adjust and cope with the lost of a loved one.

Nell Mohney says, "It is easy to focus on our problems or on what we have lost." She suggests that grief can be lifted when we change our focus, and concentrate on our assets, in other words, count our blessings (Mohney, p.32).

My emotional reaction toward Aunt Dora's death led me down the road of self-destruction. I began to welcome death as a way out of the misery that had fallen upon me. From the age of 10-12, I attempted suicide several times to escape the pain of loosing someone dear. It was painful and difficult to cope with a life filled with violence and molestation. On several occasions, I was rushed to the emergency room to have my stomach pumped. When I was revived, feelings of disappointment and despair overwhelmed me.

The best illustration that can give a glimpse of what I felt like is when a child is born without any physical contact with his/her mother. Survival is almost impossible without a mother's warm, nurturing love. I felt hopeless and grieved that my life was not worth living. There appeared to be no sign of love in my life. Suicide was very appealing. I welcomed any place other than my current environment as an improvement. Most of the time I felt depressed (nothing to smile about), condemned, and fearful. My mother's threats to send me to live with the father I never knew, or her beatings, kept me in a state of inner torment. Her threats to kick me out, when I had just moved back, were more than I could handle. The dark streets and alleys of New York City terrified me to such a degree that running away from home was not as appealing as suicide. If I ran away, I would have to return home. Whereas, suicide would end all my misery, so I thought.

In our fast-paced society, filled with numerous abandoned and abused individuals, the suicide rate is reaching monumental occurrences. Millions of people have lost hope, jobs, family members, and the courage to continue in the everyday activities of life. This suicide plague has caused many productive individuals to choose self-destruction as the remedy for coping with the grievances of this life. This human extinction, known as a form of euthanasia— a right of passage out of this world— has enticed many to exit this world through suicide (Margolis, 1985). The suicide rate among teenagers has been dramatically increasing at an alarming rate. People are unequipped to cope with the anxieties of life. Shame and rejection of family, society, God, and life has become more attractive than enduring and overcoming hardships.

Life has no meaning for those who have given up the hope of surviving. To accept suicide is to accept being labeled "mentally ill" and "irrational" by society, family, and friends (Stephenson, 1985). If this is true, the Sigmund Freud was right in his theory that suicide is ascribed to the psychological makeup of the individual. On the other hand, the theory of Emile Durkheim maintains that suicide is influenced by the social environment of the individual (Stephenson, 1985). It is no doubt both theories are true to some extent. People are self-destructing all around us. Our medical and mental institutions are flooded with people who have lost hope and purpose for the future.

Giving up on life is not the solution to solving the problems of life, I learned that the hard way. Everyone has problems, but not everyone sees suicide as the means to end all problems. In the Bible, King David went to the brink of despair, and flirted with the idea of suicide when he felt let down by God, worthless, and abandoned. He acknowledged "walking through the valley of the shadow of death" (Psalms 23:4); he felt alone like a sparrow (Psalms 107:7, 11); and looked for pity from others, but found none (Psalms 69:20). There are several Biblical accounts of others that experienced extreme depression and entertained the idea of suicide: Jonah, Elijah, Ahithophel, and Judas thought suicide would fix the problem and provide a way out. Some yielded and destroyed their lives, whereas others overcame the tendency to seek a quick escape (Wilkeson, 1978).

I think of how the Christmas Season is advertised as a time of celebration and happiness, everyone in the movies and commercial is happy with their lives and family. In reality, the Christmas holiday is a time when many people entertain the idea of suicide. During the Christmas season, the media portrays a false image that all Americans are joyful. Most of the movies aired show families traveling to visit relatives and carrying gifts. Nevertheless, this is not the true reflection of the lives of those that have been sexually abused and abandoned. This world is bursting at the seams with fields of unhappy people who are angry because no one seems to care.

Anger dealt me a hard blow when my Aunt Catherine died. Her death filled me with a bitter anger toward my mother. I blamed her for not informing me of her death.

Anger is an emotional response that mourner's experience because of the death of loved ones. My Aunt Catherine was a very special lady whom I loved dearly. She understood some of my hurt and pain. She knew many details of my life and the effects of an unloving environment had on my self-esteem. After relocating to Virginia during my teen years, I returned to New York for a visit. During this visit, I inquired about Aunt Catherine because whenever I was in town she made a special effort to see me. She made me feel very special. I was not prepared for the information about her death. I could not understand why they had done this to me, again. My family did not inform me of her condition or death.

Suddenly learning of Aunt Catherine's death caused feelings of anger to intensify as the swelled up within me. Bitterness and resentment began to inject me with its deadly venom that slowly killed the love I had for my mother. How could I forgive this oversight when my mother knew of the special bond between Aunt Catherine and me? At this point I started keeping records in my heart in a little black book; the offenses of all that hurt me were engraved in the walls of my heart. When I returned to Virginia, I purposed in my heart to ignore the biological link between my mother and me. I sentenced her to debtor's prison to be tormented until full payment was paid for all the verbal and physical abuse and abandonment that caused me unnecessary pain. Years had gone by and I refused to contact her to show any signs of love. The thought of her brought the pain of the past back to my remembrance, so I chose to forget her and erase the past.

Traveling through the *Valley of the Shadow of Death* looking for an easy way to self-destruct did not relieve my pain, nor did it provide a quick escape. It only led me to a worse place, a place I call the *Dungeon of Darkness,* or the Pit. It was a place of gross darkness in which people are held in spiritual chains of mental illness. It was not the ideal environment for a child to live. Chapter three, the dungeon experience, you will gain a greater understanding of the depth of my bitterness and how bitterness sought to set up permanent residence in my heart.

*For we wrestle not against flesh and blood,
but against...
the rulers of the darkness
of this world*

Ephesians 6:12 (KJV)

CHAPTER THREE

The Dungeon of Darkness

When you think of a dungeon, you visualize a place that is dark, spooky and cold. It gives you the creeps. This is how I felt about my next journey: it was dark, spooky, cold and terrifying. From a child's viewpoint, it was the torture chamber. My Dungeon of Darkness was the state hospital, located in New Jersey, the house of mental torment and bondage.

If you have ever seen the movie, "One Flew Over The Cuckoo's Nest," then you would have a little understanding of how the people live in the Dungeon of Darkness. The first two times I arrived at Bellevue for psychiatric treatment, I was ten and twelve years old. I was assigned to the psychiatric ward for youth or children whose parents felt they had lost control over.

A nurse took me on the grand tour of the ward. We started in the cubical room which had small 14x14 inch wooden bins arranged in a bookcase order along both facing walls. I was assigned a bin for my personal property. The tour continued to the shower room, which provided no privacy from the other patients. My first shower at Bellevue I learned how to shower with a bar of soap and no washcloth. For some strange reason, patients were not permitted to use washcloths. At Bellevue also learned how to put linen on a bed and fold and tuck the corners of the bed with hospital corners. All patients had to place linen on the bed the same way or repeat the process until those corners were perfect.

The next room was the dormitory. It was a large room filled with at least fifty beds that were packed side by side. I was informed that the suicidal patients had to move their beds nightly into the hallways of the ward for continuous surveillance. I thought, "Everyone will know why I am in here." The sleeping arrangements labeled and categorized me as suicidal with psychiatric problems. The doctor's diagnosis required heavy sedation medication to prevent any emotional outbreak or expression.

Next, Mrs. Morgan, took me down the longest hallway I had ever seen. The floors were white and they shone like glass. At the end of the hall was a large room called the Rec Room. All group gatherings took place in this room lined with barred windows that reached to the ceiling. Little did I know then that I would spend a lot of time looking out those windows onto the busy streets of New York, wondering what the future held for me?

Before entering the Rec Room, we passed a raised door with about two steps on the left corner of the hallway. This room was the Watch Tower, in which patients were continuously supervised and monitored. On special occasions, this room became the Disc Jockey's room to pipe into the Rec Room.

The final room we toured was the kitchen. It was a private room that only the privileged had access to, but primarily for hospital personnel. Once the door to the kitchen closed behind us, Mrs. Morgan instructed me not to slip and call her Aunt Catherine, but Mom Morgan. All the nurses were addressed as mom. I was pleased to find my real aunt working at the same place I was confined. I felt a sense of security knowing that Aunt Catherine was near because she knew the pain of my home life.

Bellevue became my foster home for several months. It was a temporary holding place until medical decisions were reached as to where to permanently place me. It was determined that my time was up at Bellevue and a date was set to transfer me the next home. I actually enjoyed it at Bellevue. It was better than home. The nurses and doctors were nice to you. Every night we had a graham cracker and milk snack before bed. During the day, we attended assigned art and home economics classes. I chose sewing classes to learn how to sew with a sewing machine, because my sewing was limited to hand sewing. Occasionally, we had events with other patients from another ward. When a dance was planned with the boys' ward, I enjoyed the activity of dancing to the Platters, Supremes, Temptations, and Marvin Gaye. As a teenager, I found comfort and joy in listening to the lyrics of the music of the late '50s and '60s. I could identify with messages like, "Mr. Postman," "Moon River," "Mama Said They'll Be Days Like This," "Over the Rainbow," and "Stop In The Name of Love."

The good times at Bellevue were ending. The day of my transfer from Bellevue has arrived. The attendants proceeded to put a straight jacket on me for restraining purposes, before boarding the bus. The bus was shaped like a missile, the front was pointed and the back a rounded. The windows were small and high above the ground. As I sat looking out the window, the bus traveled for miles through the city to the country. All I saw lining the highway were rows of trees and the absence of buildings. The trip seemed to take hours because of the discomfort of the straight jacket. To sit for an hour was very painful when your arms are wrapped across your chest, tightly tied around the back. I wondered what they thought I was going to do. I was not a violent or aggressive child, so why tie me up like an animal? The only violence I engaged in was self-inflicted. This I could not understand, but calmly accepted. I had given up all resistance and fight for life. I no longer cared what happened to me.

We finally arrived on the campus of my new home, the state hospital. I willingly accepted my new home because I had no place else to go. My mother signed the papers of consent to have me committed to the state hospital twice, at ten and twelve years old. She was not aware that I refused to return home to an environment of violence, verbal, physical and sexual abuse. I made it known to the medical authorities at Bellevue that if I was sent back home, I would continue to attempt suicide until I succeeded.

I thought the state hospital would be a better place than my mother's house, but the grass was not greener on the other side of the entrance doors. The attendants walked me to building 36 as if I was a violent prisoner. When the check-in procedures were finished, and all the current patients stared me down like an animal about to be hunted, I was commanded to remove all my street clothes. I did not question anything, but quickly complied. I thought since I was a kid, they would handle me with gentleness and kindness, as they did in Bellevue, but was I ever wrong. After removing my clothes, the nurse commanded me to get into the shower. Buckets of soapy water were thrown on me and I was scrubbed with a hard bristle broom as if I had fleas. I could not hold the tears back because the pain of the brush was hurting my skin as if needles where being poked into my flesh. I had never been treated so inhuman before. I wanted to return to Bellevue to be with Aunt Catherine, but I knew that was impossible. In addition, who would listen to the cry of a nut cake, for which I was labeled because of not wanting to live.

Through the tears, I could see many people, adult patients, staring at me. They sat on metal benches that lined the walls of the shower room. I felt as though I was an animal a circle of spectators who were laughing at me. When the shower ordeal ended, I was given institution clothing that resembled prison clothes. My dress had a number on the back of it and stripes. Everyone was dressed alike.

The more I was humiliated, the more my heart determined that love would not be so easy to let in this stony heart. I resolved that one would ever gain my affections.

Next was medication time. I was given a large dose of medication to control all forms of emotional expression, to smile was difficult. Everyone had to be medicated, whether they needed it or not. Medication was a part of the treatment and you accepted what they gave you without complaint. If I tried to hide the pill under my tongue, I did not succeed. Everyone's mouth was thoroughly checked to make sure the pills were swallowed.

One time when I was medicated, the nurse escorted me to the dormitory and showed me my assigned bed, which was in the first dormitory, near the center aisle and doorway. I scanned the large room filled with beds equally spaced, and noticed the metal grates that covered the windows. There was no way of ever escaping this place.

After leaving the dormitory, I was escorted to the "Day Room." It was a large room with shiny floors, a television with a group of chairs facing it, tables and chairs set up for games, a porch with thick bars, doors that locked with a skeleton key, and a glass wall covering the nurses' station. In this room, most of the patients spent a large portion of the day. I noticed patients screaming and talking out of their head, while some crouched in a corner banging their heads onto the wall. Some patients walked back and forth talking and answering themselves. You know you have lost your mind when you answer yourself. This was truly the nut house and I had no way out.

At dinnertime, we were rounded up like cattle and marched through an underground tunnel. It was dark and cold in the tunnel and I was very frightened, but knew I had better not show any signs of emotion. Therefore, I counseled myself to bury my fears and bit my lip and nails until we arrived in the lightened room at the end. It was amazing how bright the light was in the cafeteria after leaving the darkness of the tunnel behind me. We were seated at assigned tables and told the rules. Everything, the bed, clothing, medication, and seating were assigned. You had to eat everything on your tray. Eating tapioca pudding became a battle for me because it resembled vomit. I hated the taste and texture of it in my mouth, but I was not about to find out what would happen if I did not eat all of my food. I was warned that I would not be permitted to eat the rest of the day if I did not eat all of my food, nor would I get television privileges.

After the meal was over, back to the dark tunnel to our building and ward. When we returned from the cafeteria, it was medication and naptime. Patients who had been there for awhile had special passes to roam the grounds and visit the store and snack bar. You gained this honor after sixty days of compliance and no emotional outbursts. I was new and the second and only kid of the ward. Therefore, it would be a long time before I would be allowed such freedom.

I spent a lot of time singing all the songs I could remember that were learned from "American Band Stand" and the popular hits of the late '50s and early '60s. I believe singing protected me from going insane. The barred porch became the place I did my singing and daydreaming. I would spend hours staring at the trees and fantasize of another world and place where love was welcome.

The *Dungeon of Darkness* was my home for several years. The nurses began to show favoritism toward me. The head nurse, Ms. English, would take me to work in the garden at her house in Englewood, NJ. When I first met Ms. English, I was afraid to breathe around her. I thought she was mean, but she turned out to be a nice, caring person. She and Ms. Delaney were two of my favorite nurses. I could tell that they thought I should not have been put into such a place. There was rumors' going around the hospital that someone was trying to adopt me. I heard my psychiatrist, who had lost her family in a concentration camp, was trying to adopt me, and that a nurse wanted to adopt me. Nothing ever materialized from these rumors. I had to remain in the house of bondage until my mother released me.

At 16, I decided it was time to be free from the *Dungeon of Darkness*, so I planned an escape. I was caught and placed in confinement in a room without windows. I was bound in sheets that attached my wrist and ankles together behind my back and placed on a cold floor. My medication was increased to 250 mg of Thorazine. I remember floating down the hallway to use the bathroom and foaming at my mouth. The medication made me feel like a zombie. Surely, I would be no more trouble.

Time passed and the incident were forgotten. I gained privileges that permitted me to roam the grounds. One day I took advantage of the freedom and began to plot another escape. The warnings echoed in my mind of the punishment given to those who attempted to escape and how they would be transferred to building 60, which was called the snake pit. The reports about building 60 frightened me to the point that I was determined to succeed at my escape. I heard that the nurses beat you bad for no reason in building 60. I could not handle that kind of pain. It would only remind me of the brutal beatings I had received from my mother.

Once I drank a bottle of Clorox bleach to take my life and my mother found out. I will never forget her words: "You want to die? It took nine months to bring you here, but I'll kill you in nine minutes." The beating she gave me felt as though she was going to succeed. She beat my bare skin with an extension cord. I jumped into the bathtub for safety and was beaten out of it until I surrendered to the pain and took the blows because there was no place to run. My 90 pounds were no match for my mother, who was talk and big boned. No more beatings for me, not from my mother or nurses. I was fed up with people hurting me when I did nothing wrong to deserve such cruelty.

The day of escape finally arrived. I ran away by hiding in the back of a van that would eventually leave for the city. I laid still and waited in silence. The engine started and the driver made it through the main gate check. I was on my way to be free at last from the house of bondage, the *Dungeon of Darkness.*

When the van came to a complete stop, I was in New York City, a few blocks from my mother's house. I knew the police would be looking for me for the next 72 hours. If I were caught, I would be returned to Bellevue and then back to the state hospital. I made up my mind that I would never go back, but I got exactly what I feared.

The police apprehended me and took me to the 30th Precinct for instructions as to where I was to be held in custody. A miracle was waiting for me at the precinct. My psychiatrist sent a letter of release with the comment that all I needed was love, not psychiatric treatment. I was released into my mother's custody for a few months until an opportunity opened for me to travel to Virginia, my *Land of Canaan*. This *Land of Canaan* was located in the city of Newport News and Hampton, Virginia. In chapter four, I will share how my heart and soul were transformed by the power of God, which filled me with the desire to forgive those that abused and abandoned me.

For the Lord Your God
is bringing you into a good
land....a land where bread
will not be scarce and
you will lack nothing

Deuteronomy 8:7-9 (NIV)

CHAPTER FOUR

The Land of Canaan

It was the July 4 weekend in 1966 when I arrived in Newport News, Virginia. I was employed as the babysitter for the couple I traveled with, to care for their toddler. Taking this job made it possible for me to receive an expense-paid trip to a place I had never visited. I had not planned to make Virginia my home, but the southern hospitality and friendliness of the people made me want to remain in the South. As I sat on the porch, passersby spoke as they walked by your house.

The neighborhood was so peaceful and quiet; I could hear the crickets in the night silence. There were no siren sounds or any loud music playing in the streets to drown out the voices of nature, nor did bright city lights flood out the starry host that decorated the dark sky. It was customary to recline on the glider on a summer night to enjoy family conservation. My first time on the glider I was hesitant because of the way it moved like a swing, but once I faced the fear of sitting on this unusual swing, and sat down, I found it relaxing and fun.

On Sundays, we went to the local Baptist church. It was my first time attending an all African-American church. I grew up Catholic in a mixed congregation of people from all races. I was amazed at the attire of the women; it was like a fashion show of mink coats, hats, and fancy outfits. The preaching was in English and not Latin. I could understand what the preacher was saying. In the Catholic Church before the language changed, the major portion of the service was in Latin, and even the congregational responses were in Latin.

My first reaction to the South was a cultural shock. The piercing quiet and lack of evening activity and noise made it feel and sound like a ghost town. However, I quickly adjusted to the quiet lifestyle of the Virginians. I began to like the neighborhood and friendly neighbors. Most of the neighbors were educated professionals who attended church every Sunday. The family in the adjacent house impressed me. Their names were the Scotts, of whom I heard were wealthy. Their son Bobby eventually became a senator.

I liked what I saw and desired a similar lifestyle, but it seemed like an impossible dream. I had neither family nor anyone willing to invest in my future to mentor me into a secure life. If my life was going to improve, it was going to be up to me. I took immediate action and informed my mother that I would not be returning to New York.

She was enraged by my insubordinate attitude. She threatened to have me returned home by calling the police. I was 16 years old when I ran away and left New York. My mother's threats were to no avail to the couple acting as my illegal guardians, because they knew my home situation and showed me compassion and sympathy.

I continued to ignore my mother's threats, as David ignored the threats of Goliath to defy the army of Israel. I began to build a new life in Virginia. I began to climb the ladder of success by taking advantage of every employment opportunity. My first few jobs were for minimum wages of 90 cents an hour as a waitress, factory worker and dry cleaner's clerk. The next job was in a bag factory cuffing large burlap bags with plastic liners. I continued working low wage jobs until I found something more secure that provided opportunities for advancement. In 1968, a better paying job opened with General Electric Television Division. I worked on the assembly line, checking the electrical cord of the television for damage. I soon advanced to working as a trouble shooter and quality control inspector. In addition, General Electric provided educational assistance that made it possible for me to advance my education.

My dream was to go to finish high school and go on to college. However, because I did not have the privilege of a high school education, it was difficult to believe that dreams could come true. The giants of negativism threatened daily to defy the possibilities that I could be a winner. I became hopeful toward the future as my dream became stronger.

Over the course of three years, I climbed from waitress and factory worker to running an engineering photo lab. As a photo lab technician, I was able to take evening college preparatory courses after completing my GED diploma with tuition reimbursement upon obtaining a passing grade. I was later admitted into an associates degree program in photography with a minor in commercial art at Thomas Nelson Community College.

For the next eleven years I worked two jobs and went to college in the evening. I developed a love for the college atmosphere. I was excited when I realized that I could conquer the giants of my past and kill all the negative words that built up strongholds in my mind. There seemed to be a special energy that filled every classroom. I felt motivated to excel and become a top adult student. I found myself making a commitment to take some type of class that I might continuously gain knowledge.

My completion of junior high school was interrupted by many devastating childhood experiences. Living in a large family of eight children with only a single parent offered very few educational opportunities. I became one of the statistics of junior high school dropouts. Yet, in my heart I longed to graduate from high school because that seemed to be the only way toward self-advancement.

When I was a child, going to school was the only way to escape the abuse and violence of my home. I loved going to school because I got recognition for my academic performance. At the end of the school day, the fear of what I would face when I arrived home tormented my mind.

Remembering the crisis that halted my formal education, it seemed foolish and impossible to pursue a college education in my twenties. However, after completing my GED in my early twenties, I realized that I wanted more than just a high school equivalence certificate.

When I enrolled in college and began to accumulate 35 credits with a 3.7 GPA, my confidence grew. In addition, my professors and associates began to encourage me to finish college. Their words of encouragement helped me take possession of the promise land, the *Land of Canaan*. However, my self-esteem was still low. Although on the surface it appeared as if I was positive and happy, I felt defeat and despair within. I could not seem to break out of the negative mentality of seeing myself deficient of the necessary abilities to excel. Somehow there remained an emptiness and void within me that I could not understand. To the spectator my life looked well put together, but behind closed doors I was unraveled and coming apart. I thought, " I should be happy, I have a good paying job, I am in college. I have a beautifully decorated apartment in a nice community and a new car. Even though men line up to get a date with me, I am struggling with my self-worth." I am realizing that education and material possessions do not make you happy, so I questioned how does a person find happiness.

These questions continued to plague me so that I could not sleep. I sought to find comfort through church involvement. I remember attending 12:00 noon mass at the local Catholic Church looking for answers in the beauty of the stain glass and religious statues that decorated the church. I would site a variety of prayers for each bead on my rosary beads and continued to feel great emptiness. I inquired of the priest if I could join the choir and was discouraged by the thick set of documents that had to be filled out. I left the church in deep hunger and embarked on a search for significance and contentment. This was the beginning of my pilgrimage.

A religious pilgrimage is a unique, personal account of experiences in a Christian's journey through life. My pilgrimage began January 1979, when I experienced the transforming love of Jesus Christ. I was invited to a non-denominational church where I heard the gospel. I left the church with the words of a loving God echoing in my mind and disrupting my sleep.

I began to understand why the emptiness and void feelings that I had been experiencing lately were so strong. It was the Spirit of God drawing me to Himself through Jesus Christ. The truth was that only Jesus Christ could produce happiness in my life, through accepting the gift of salvation. On the next Sunday, I asked Jesus into my heart and acknowledged that I was a sinner and in need of a Savior. A floodgate opened in my heart and the tears poured like a waterfall from my eyes. During that time, I realized how much I desired a father to love me and make the pain go away. Now, I have an invisible father in which I could carry all hurts too. I felt as if I was a child meeting her real father for the first time. I began to tell him about the abuse and abandonment, and the side effects that continue to produce pain. When I left the altar, I was a changed woman. Something on the inside of me changed. The sun reflected a beauty I had never beheld before Jesus changed me. Somehow, I knew something had happened within my heart. I became hungry and thirsty for knowledge about this Jesus, who took my place on the cross.

In pursuit of understanding salvation from sin and eternal death, I began to search the scriptures for a greater understanding of the will of God for my life. Attending Sunday school and worship service increased my understanding of God's love and forgiveness. The thought that I was chosen by God, my Creator, to fulfill his plan gave my life purpose and meaning.

After reading the story about the children of Israel and the land of Canaan, I started to adopt the command to go up and possess the land as a direct command from God to me. I saw the land of Canaan as the promise land, a place of restoration of everything that the devil stole, killed and destroyed in my life. I accepted the challenge to become excellent in whatever I was given to do. With faith in God as my guide, I believed the best of Canaan, the abundant life, was yet to come. All sufficiency in all the things I needed to live for the Lord was possible through Jesus Christ, the source of all provisions. The *Land of Canaan* became the place in which my spirit was born again, my soul was restored, and my mind renewed. I began to believe that the impossible was possible. If the Lord went to fight the battles for the children of Israel to possess the promised land, then he would do the same for whoever would take Him at his word. He shows no favoritism to anyone. As I held onto the promise of a fruitful life, I became aware of the principle of forgiveness.

As freely as I had been forgiven, I must forgive. Jesus laid the foundation of the prerequisite of forgiveness. He said, "If you forgive men when they sin against you, your heavenly Father will also forgive you. But if you do not forgive men their sins, your Father will not forgive your sins" (Matthew 6:14-15). The teachings of Jesus commanded me to forgive in order to grow spiritually. Forgiveness became the key that opened the door to my healing.

Yvette as an infant. *Yvette's toddler years.*

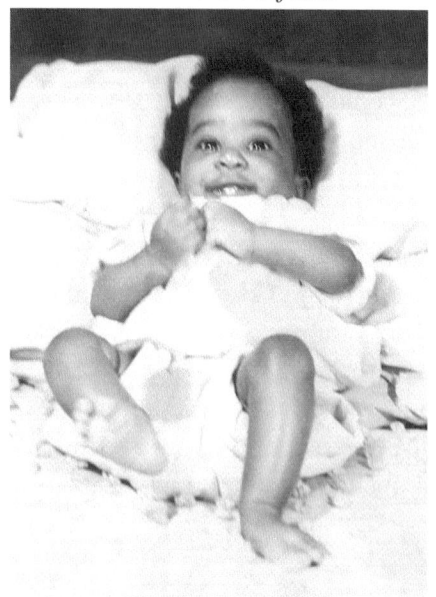

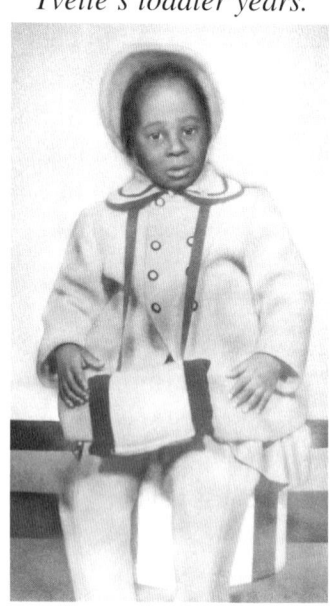

Yvette as a young girl.  *Yvette in her early teen years.*

"Delight yourself in the Lord and He will give you the desire of your heart."
Psalm 37:4

Yvette's wedding day. - A real Cinderella.

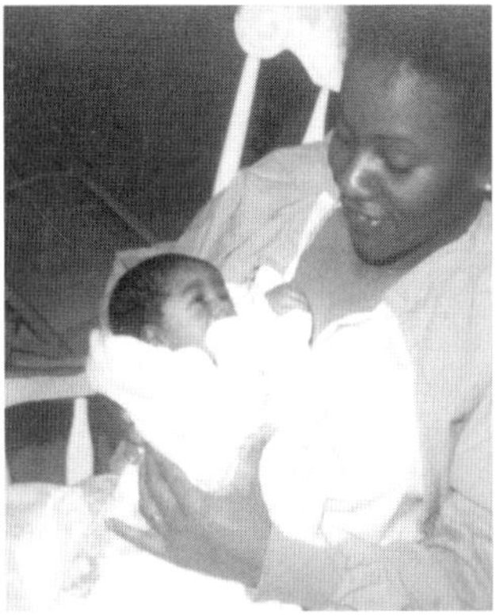

A barren woman becomes a joyful mother of children.

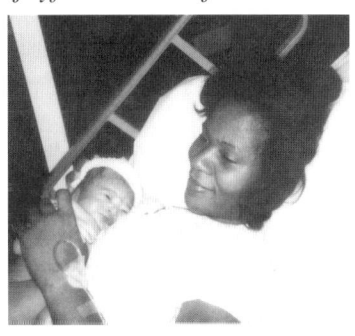

Yvette's graduation day.
It is never too late for dreams to come true.

Jehava and Twila

Put off your old
self which was
being corrupted
by its sinful desires
to be made new
in the attitude
of your mind

Ephesians 4:22-23 (NIV)

CHAPTER FIVE

A Winning Attitude

The first thing most people ask me is "How can you forgive people for those horrible things they did to you and not become bitter?" My first response is, "I was *freely* forgiven, how could I give any less?" The desire to forgive did not develop overnight, nor was it willingly embraced, but it took a number of years. There was a constant battle within my mind to hold onto the black book that listed the wrongs others had done to me and never destroy it. The black book was the only evidence and record I could use that gave justification for not loving others the way I was loved by Christ. Unconditional love was out of the question. My mind continuously demanded payment. I worried that if I covered others' wrongs with love, they would get off easy and not have to pay the debt owned me. However, the more I read the Bible, the more I realized that there is no acceptable excuse for unforgiveness.

The story of the unmerciful servant in Matthew 18:21-35 clarified any misconception I may have had concerning forgiveness. Reading this passage I saw that Peter asked the same question that I had asked in my heart: "Lord, how many times shall I forgive…up to seven times?" Jesus answered, " I tell you not seven times, but seventy-seven times." Hearing these words, I knew I would not be keeping count. If there was any confusion about forgiveness, this illustration will provide a clearer understanding: The kingdom of heaven is like a king who wanted to settle accounts with his servants. As he began the settlement, a man who owed him…was brought to him. Since he was not able to pay, the master ordered that he, his wife, his children, and all that he had be sold to repay the debt. The servant fell on his knees before him, "Be patient with me," he begged, "and I will pay back everything."

The servant's master took pity on him, canceled the debt and let him go. But when that servant went out, he found one of his fellow servants that owed him…He grabbed him and began to choke him. "Pay back what you owe me!" He demanded. His fellow servant fell on his knees and begged, "Be patient with me, and I will pay you back." However, he refused. Instead, he went off and had the man thrown into prison until he could pay the debt. When the other servants saw what had happened, they were greatly distressed, went, and told their master everything that had happened. Then the master called the servant in. "You wicked servant, " he said, "I canceled all that debt of yours because you begged me to. Shouldn't you have had mercy on your fellow servant just as I had on you?" In anger, his master turned him over to the jailers to be tortured until he should pay back all he owed. This is how my heavenly Father will treat each of you unless you forgive…from your heart.

No matter how cruelly I have been treated, I am required to overcome evil with good by forgiving as often as it takes to free myself and others from the torture of debts that are impossible to pay back.

It took years to win the battle of my mind as it sought to hold onto the offenses and make others pay. I struggled with reflections of the past that continued to remind me of the pain I had experienced as a child. I often felt as if I was in "The Twilight Zone," challenging the stability of my mind and the word of God. Often the past became like a giant demanding that I remember all those fearful sights. During times of weakness, I found myself embracing the pain by wearing a robe of self-pity and self-condemnation. The victim's cry often filled my heart with pleads for help and relief, but no human find no one to deliver and heal me from the scars of the past.

One day I read Isaiah 52:1-2, "Awake, Awake…clothe yourself with strength. Put on your garments of splendor…Shake yourself from the chains on your neck, O captive daughter." It was as if these words were for me. They were piercing and powerful, reaching down to the root of my soul and discerning my thoughts. The enemy of my mind, Satan, was out to sift me of the new life I had found in Christ. He was using the reflections of the past to steal, kill, and destroy any future hope of ever becoming a healed woman.

If the battle to forgive was going to be won, I had to make the choice to apply the word of God and allow it to convert my attitude from a losing to *A Winning Attitude*. It was time to learn a new way of thinking, to replace the negative sayings of the devil for the positive positive sayings of Jesus. It was time to get rid of poisonous thinking that kept the garbage of my past smelling. It was to stop maintaining a victim's consciousness. Instead, I must find the best solution, one that would instill hope for the future. Ralph Waldo Emerson said, "What lies behind us and what lies before us are my tiny matter compared to what lies within us. According to Zig Ziglar, "Your attitude is more important than your aptitude." Many doctors, lawyers, educators, and salespeople have agreed that your attitude is the key to a successful life. Perhaps it is best to say that your attitude determines the level of your success. William James, the father of psychology, supported this idea when he said, "The most important discovery of our time is that we can alter our lives by altering our attitudes."

I began to believe that it was not impossible for me to be set free from the mindset that I had been stuck in for so many years. I was not condemned to be imprisoned with garbage thinking, but I could choose to reconstruct my mind to reflect dreams of the future and not dreads of the past.

I remember on a drive to Virginia Beach, there was a certain park with a beautiful grassy covered hill that ran along Interstate 44 in Virginia. It was called Mount Trashmore. My husband, a Virginian, told me the history behind the construction of the hill and park. The hill in Mount Trashmore once was a trash dump called the Virginia Beach Dump. Someone purchased the land, covered the trash with dirt and seeded it with grass, put a fense around it and named it Mount Trashmore. This is similar to what happened to my mind. A man name Jesus purchased a temple that once served as a human dumping ground, and covered it with love. His love nurtured and beautified my life. Then, he built a hedge around it with His Spirit's presence and renamed it the Temple of God. The apostle Paul confirmed this illustration when he said; "Do you not know that your body is the temple of the Holy Spirit, who is in you, whom you have received from God? You are not your own, you were bought at a price"(I Corinthians 6:19).

According to Zig Ziglar, "The mind is a dutiful servant and will follow the instructions we give it." My mind was trained to believe the "I Can'ts" when it came to facing new challenges. I noticed that my words reflected what I had stored up and believed in my heart. Jesus said, "Out of the overflow of the heart, the mouth speaks" (Matthew 12:34). Negatives thinking often made me feel downcast, depressed and defeated, whenever I gave into these feelings. I believed what I felt was real and was greatly afflicted.

Meditating on the Psalms of David encouraged me not to give up, but know that someone else has overcome such emotions. I gained comfort knowing that King David experienced similar emotional struggles when he said, "Be at rest once more, O my soul, for the Lord has been good to you. For you, O Lord, have delivered my soul from death, my eyes from tears, my feet from stumbling, that I may walk before the Lord in the land of the living" (Psalms 116:7-10).

Through the power of prayer, reading and memorizing the scriptures, and applying the life changing principles, I was able to witness the result of a newly constructed attitude. I became more positive and hopeful about the future. I believed that I had a new way of thinking about life and its challenges, and that the past should not limit advancement of the future. The excitement of a new me with a new lease on life empowered me to see myself as a victor of the assaults of the past.

An intense hunger increased my appetite to understand the mind renewal process, so I read everything I could get my hands on. Books like *As A Man Thinketh,* by James Allen and Acres of

Diamonds are two of my favorites. A suggested reading and auto tape recording list can be found in the back of this book if you are serious about changing your attitude.

Over the years, my mind took on a new outlook on life, one that became more positive. This is not to say that I never felt down, discouraged, but that whenever such attacks came, I would reach for uplifting literature, or resources that helped me refocus. It is when our focus turns toward self that the doors of our mind are opened to the Prince of the Power of the Air of Negativism. He will dump garbage into our minds, if we give him a foothold, with the sole purpose of stealing, killing, and destroying our lives.

In *See You At The Top,* Zig Ziglar says, "You are what you are and where you are because of what has gone into your mind. You can change what you are and where you are by changing what goes into your mind." In 1979, when I married Joseph Jones, my desire for a college education changed to wanting to be like the Proverbs 31 woman. The passion and desire to finish college was stored into the vault of my dreams and replaced by a new passion, to learn how to be a godly wife. After the excitement of the new birth experience in Christ and marriage had worn off, the need for personal development increased so that I began to think of returning to school or having children.

I had begun to set goals by writing them down in the form of a prayer list. I set deadlines next to each goal. The desire for children outweighed the desire for education, but I was faced with the impossibility of having children. It was medically diagnosed that I would never conceive because of the childhood experience of rape. Yet, I had a new mind that believed in miracles, if I only had a mustard seed of faith in the promise that, "He settles the barren woman in her home as a happy mother of children" (Psalms 113:9). I stood on these words and prayed them until it became a reality that I, a barren woman, would truly conceive. I delivered my first child on May 7, 1981 and my second child was born on August 17, 1984. By then I was fully persuaded that what God had promised, He was able also to perform. Only God was able to renew my mind by the power of His Spirit that I might approach life's challenges and crisis with the mind of Christ. I began to believe I could obtain a college education, as I had believed to become a mother. The dream of completing college seems to be a mission possible.

In 1989, I enrolled in college to complete an associate's degree program. By 1992, I graduated with an Associate in Arts degree. The dream to receive a college education came true in my early forties. This accomplishment was exhilarating but not completely satisfactory because another dream was taking form in my heart. I wanted to further my education and earn a bachelor's degree.

Meditating on, "Do you believe...then according to your faith will it be done" (Matthew 9:28-29). The positive words of Jesus to the two blind men that sought restoration of their sight became the words that I stored in my heart. I professed these words until I marched across the stage on May 1994, to receive the Bachelor of Science degree.

I believe these examples will help you understand the truth that "As a man or woman thinks, so are they" (Proverbs 23:7). You cannot think one way and speak another. Jesus said, "Make a tree good and its fruit will be good, or make a tree bad and its fruit will be bad, for a tree is recognized by its fruit. For out of the overflow of the heart the mouth speaks. The good man brings good things out of the good stored up in him, and the evil man brings up evil things out of the evil stored up in him" (Matthew 12:33-35).

First things first, make the decision to store up the good treasures of the positive sayings of Jesus Christ, the only words on earth that are powerful enough to renew your mind and change your view of life. Your life can be whatever you want it to be, if you adopt the kind of thinking that will produce the abundant life. Christ made the difference in my life. He gave me the desire to seek *A Winning Attitude* through trusting Him to transform my mind. My past view of life and of other people was filled with suspicion and negativism. I did not believe in miracles, nor that it was possible for my life to change; yet, change did transpire. Still, it did not happen over night, nor was it based on a religious formula. It took years of discipline, prayer and faith in what God said that was mine. I made the choice to see myself through my Heavenly Father's eyes possessing the dreams of my heart and making a difference in the lives of others. I no longer agreed with the lies of Satan, that I was bound for life in the chains of the past. Jesus' death broke those chains and liberated me that I may enjoy life more abundantly. As David Schwartz has put it, "People are not measured in inches, or pounds, or college degrees, or family background; they are measured by the size of their thinking." How big we think determines the range of our accomplishments.

To renew your mind choose to withdraw only the positive and good thoughts from the depository of our memory bank. Practice and focus on what the Apostle Paul said, " Whatever things are true, whatever things are admirable or praiseworthy, think about such things (Phillipians 4:8). Following the principles in this chapter will give you the confidence and courage to overcome the devil's schemes. Remember that the devil is a thief. He has come to steal, kill, and destroy your freedom. Giving forgiveness is the key to freeing you and others. Your freedom is directly tied to how much you give forgive. Think: "What kind of world would this world be if everyone in it were unforgiving and held onto every grudge?" *Why forgive* anyway, since it only lets the offender off the hook. It is my desire that the next chapter will give you understanding as to why it is important to forgive.

One final word on cultivating *A Winning Attitude*: the mind is like a camera. If I hold a camera in my hands and take pictures, it records whatever I focus the lens, (eye) on. Once the image is recorded, I can choose whether I want to develop that image into a photograph or not. I do not have to store the film away and look at it several times to reflect on the images. I can be selective and focus on those images that enlighten and encourage. The same is true of what we choose to replay on the screen of our mind. If I focus on the negative and painful images of the past and continuously meditate on those images, change would never occur in the way I think. Painful images can steal, kill and destroy hope for the future. Our minds are made up of photographic images, recorded through our eyes, whether good or bad, but you and I have a God given free will to choose what to focus our mental energy on. Keep in mind, "Thoughts become words; words become actions; actions become habits; habits become character; and character becomes destiny" (Charles Plunkett).

*Forgive us our debts
as we also have
forgiven
our debtors*

Matthew 6:12 (NIV)

CHAPTER SIX

Why Forgive?

"Forgive? Are you serious? After all the hurt and pain they caused me? He raped me and stole my self worth! He brutally beat me in front of the children."

"Forgive her? She gave me up for adoption because I was in the way. She abandoned me and put me in the custody of the state. I didn't ask to come into this world!"

"Forgive him? He was my father and he raped me when I trusted him."

"Why should I forgive her? She falsely accused me of having an affair with her husband! I thought she trusted me.

"I can never forgive how she took advantage of my generosity and hospitality! She took my car without permission me and ran my telephone bill up to $400."

"How could a fair God expect me to forgive them for wrecking my life? It is not fair that they do not have to pay for what they have done to me. It is because of being molested, raped, rejected and abandoned that I tasted the bitter waters of a life that dealt me an undeserved blow. I learned to hate myself and life because of the unfair treatment and abusive treatment of what others have done to me."

"After 30 years of, he doesn't want to be married anymore, and I have to be the one to forgive? Come on! God cannot be that unjust! He knows how I faithfully served and supported him while he reached his career goals. He is the one who filed for divorce, not me."

"He cheated on me and slept with my best friend. I worked while he finished medical school, and this is how he repays me."

The list is endless of the statements of abused and abandoned victims who find it difficult to forgive those who marred their lives. Our society is filled with wounded people who have experienced similar ordeals.

I have heard these statements over the past twenty years from people who suffered from some form of abuse and were left abandoned with emotional scars. I have encountered the tears of many women and heard their cry for relief from the pain. Listen to some of those cries, and perhaps you will understand the depth of their pain. Teenagers have cried over the sexual assaults inflicted upon them by trusted ones; women have cried of the unfaithfulness of their husbands; and men have cried silently over the abandonment of their wives. What makes these confessions so grievous is that many of these sufferers are Christians. This is a great tragedy. Too many people are captives of an invisible prison of emotional and mental torment.

Overcoming the pain seems impossible. Children are crying for help and relief from the pain of sexual abuse. Daughters are crying because their mothers and fathers have either abused or abandoned them. I felt that this book on my life's journey in the wilderness will encourage, comfort, inspire, and motivate others to believe that they, too, can climb the Mount Everest in their lives and overcome the bitter climate of unforgiveness. It is through understanding and experiencing forgiveness that freedom from the past can be achieved. I do not know what your story is, or whether perhaps you are working with someone who has been abused, but I do know that forgiveness frees.

Maybe your mother does not love you as she loves your other siblings, or maybe your marriage partner abandoned you for another. Maybe your child or loved one died a premature death by the hands of another, or maybe you spent your life in a foster home or orphanage and now you are filled with hostility and bitterness. The answer to your may be found in the art of forgiveness. You may need to forgive those who hurt you.

You may feel you have the right to feel the way you do because she/he abused you and caused you pain. You are not the only one who has held onto such thinking. Holding onto the pain of the past can often lead to deep depression. Whenever we say we have the right to hold onto bitterness, resentment, and hatred, we are on the road to a depressive future of tormenting emotional bondage. If you surrender the weights of injustice to the Lord, He will free you from the yoke of unforgiveness. He is the only one who can heal your wounded heart and replace your sadness with joy.

Another way to free yourself from the chains of an unforgiving spirit is to "Never take vengeance into your own hands, my dear friends: stand back and let God punish if He will. For it is written: 'Vengeance belongs to Me: I will repay...If your enemy hungers, feed him; if he is thirsty, give him something to drink.' Do not allow yourself to be overpowered with evil. Take the offensive- overpower evil with good!" (Romans 12:19-21) It is God's business to judge and repay those who hurt you; nevertheless, He invites you to join him in His work of forgiveness and loving the unlovable. "Be kind, tender hearted one to another, forgiving one another, "as God would say it- "even as I for Christ's sake have forgiven you" (Eph. 4:32)

You may be thinking, forgiving those who hurt you would not be fair since you had to go through so much pain because of their actions. You say within yourself, "Why should I just let them go free? They have not even had the common decency to apologize and admit they did wrong. By holding onto this attitude I increased the anger I felt within my heart. This provided me the necessary excuse to be in control. It was not appealing to give up this control easily. Yet, I knew I could not experience freedom until I let go of the offense and freed the offender with the keys of forgiveness. I began to understand that forgiveness frees me to love, as God has loved me. I was forgiven that I might be forgiving. Forgiveness is love in action.

One day the opportunity to apply what I had learned about forgiveness presented itself when I called my mother and asked her to forgive me for failing to accept her as she was. Christ looked beyond my faults and saw my need for love and forgiveness;

should I offer any less? As I continued talking, I could hear her voice breaking up as the tears began to flow. My heart flooded with compassion and love that came down from heaven, because of myself I was unable to express such love. From that moment, forgiveness removed the ocean of bitterness and hatred from between us. Why forgive? Forgiveness is the bridge leading to hope for the future and unconditional love.

I know for many of you, forgiving the awful things others have done to you is hard; believe me, it is very hard, if not almost impossible for you to forgive. In fact, the truth is, you cannot forgive. It is humanly impossible for you to forgive anyone without the Lord's power. Although we have been given a free will to choose to forgive, forgiveness can only be accomplished by God himself, working forgiveness in us, through Jesus Christ. When we exercise obedience to God's commandment to forgive, we allow the Holy Spirit to begin the ongoing process of forgiveness to begin. Keep in mind that forgiveness is not a one-time event, but a continual process that is repeated throughout our life on earth. As long as we are in contact with people, offenses will come and forgiveness will follow. Someone will say or do something daily that will rub you the wrong way and cause you to become offended. This is why Jesus said to forgive seventy times seven, meaning continuously. Kay Scott says, "Forgiveness is a process that is accomplished after enough of the anger has been forfeited and at least some healing has taken place. It should not be expected to happen too soon." A wise man once said, "There is a time to every purpose under heaven." (Ecclesiastes 3:1) I believe there is a time that everyone must make the choice to forgive on a daily basis and not to hold any grudges. Live a life of Jubilee, forgive the debts of those who owe you and mark the record, "Paid In Full." Every day of our lives is an opportunity to live in Jubilee.

Eventually someone will offend you and cause you pain, but what you do with that pain determines the level of freedom you enjoy.

There is nothing easy about forgiveness when we are still hurting from the wounds that have been inflicted upon us. It is my belief that the only way to cope with this pain is to give it to the Lord and trust Him to heal your damaged emotions. It is okay to be honest and pour out your heart to Him. Tell Him how you feel and what hurts, because He knows, but desires you to recognize Him as the only source of your help and healing. When I read, "Though my father and mother forsake (abandon) me, the Lord will receive (adopt) me," I gained a sense of belonging. I felt that someone really cared how I felt. God has a plan for all of our lives, a good plan, one that gives hope for the future, not a plan to harm us, a new life plan. New life is possible only through forgiveness. There is no life without forgiveness.

I believe forgiveness is the first step toward wholeness and healing. It is through forgiveness that the bridge of love is built. Letting go of the bitterness and taking hold of love is the consummation of my journey to forgiveness. I chose to let God repay those who offended me and allow His love to flow through me.

I have not apprehended all knowledge and understanding about the lifelong process of forgiveness, but I know that forgiveness freed me from the torments of the past. I no longer had to pursue my offenders to pay for the wrongs done to me. It is unjust to expect payment for something that could not be repaid. By choosing to release the "black book," the record account of those who wronged, to the Lord, I have been able to enjoy a peace that goes beyond human understanding. This peace is available to all that will choose to let go of the pain and let God heal with a touch of love. I know of no other way to start the journey to forgiveness other than becoming a vehicle in which love can travel.

If I could close this chapter with a guarantee of winning triumphantly over all the pain of being a victim of sexual abuse and abandonment, I would, but I would be leading you on the wrong journey. The journey of unforgiveness is controlled by the dictates of the flesh and leads to frustration, confusion, and resentment. Choosing to forgive has given me peace with God and myself. No longer do I hate myself nor seek self-destructive methods to escape the life. My mission is to challenge you, the reader, to recognize the power of forgiveness and accept God's love as the only pursuit to toward wholeness. It is my desire to cover the unloved with God's love land to allow love to bind up the broken hearted and heal their wounds. My prayer is that *The Pursuit of Love* encourages and enlightens you to believe that the truth of God's love will set you free to love the unlovable. May God comfort you with these truths and encourage you to share this story of a search for love with those held captive by the stronghold of self-hatred.

Yvette Jones

Yvette with her family: Twila, Jehava, and husband, Joe.

Yvette Jones is a gifted, enthusiastic, motivational and retreat speaker. She is the spouse of Dr. Joseph Jones. Yvette is the Director of Corporate Relations for the Samuel Morris Scholars Program at Taylor University. She is a member of the board of directors for the Fort Wayne Rescue Mission, the Fort Wayne Sexual Assault and Treatment Center, the Career Development Professionals of Indiana, the National Association for Female Executives, the Early Childhood Alliance and the Crisis Pregnancy Center. She has previously served as a member of the Leadership Council at Brookside Community Church, the Fort Wayne Civic Theatre Guild and board of directors of the Fort Wayne Civic Theatre. She has been voted into Who's Who among professionals and the National Association for Female Executives in 1998, 1999, and 2000.

She is the owner of Virtuous Creations, a business that specializes in porcelain ethnic dolls and portrait like dolls.

Yvette and her husband, Joseph, are the parents of two daughters, Twila, who sophomore is at Taylor University, Upland and Jehava, a junior at Blackhawk Christian High School.

Her education includes: Communications, Commercial Art, Photography, Humanities, African American Studies, Human Resource Management, Real Estate, Fund Raising, and porcelain doll making.

My mission is to challenge all to pursue the One who can make their dreams come true, the One who can enable them to reach their full potential, the One who can heal their broken heart and bind up their wounds that they may become the best for His glory and honor.

Resource References

Bierker, Susan B. *About Sexual Abuse.*
Illinois: Charles C. Thomas Publisher, 1989.
Finkelhor, David *A Sourcebook On Child Sexual Abuse.*
Newbury Park: Sage Publications, 1986.
Geiser, Robert L. *Hidden Victims: The Sexual Abuse of Children.*
Boston: Beacon Press, 1979.
Allen, James *As A Man Thinketh.*
New York: Grosset & Dunlap
Ziglar, Zig *See You At The Top.*
Gretna: Pelican Publishing Company, 1976.
New International Bible
Mohney, Nell W. *How To Be Up On Down Days.* Nashville: Dimensions For Living, 1997.
Margolis, Otto S. *Loss, Grief, and Bereavement: A Guide for Counseling.* New York: Praeger, 1985.
Wilkerson, David. *Suicide.* Texas: Wilkerson Publications, 1978.
Stephenson, John S. *Death, Grief, and Mourning.* New York: The Free Press, 1985

For information on scheduling Yvette Jones to speak for your event, please contact Speak Up Speaker Services toll free at (888) 870-7719 or e-mail Speakupinc@aol.com or check their website at: www.SpeakUpSpeakerServices.com

Order Form

Yvette M. Jones

THE PURSUIT OF LOVE

$10.00 per book
plus $3.00 shipping and handling

Name _____

Address _____

City _____ ST _____ Zip _____

Phone (____) _____ Fax (____) _____

               ___ Books @ $10.00 each _____
Shipping and handling ($3.00 ea.) _____
Total enclosed _____

___ Check # _____   ___ Money Order
___ Credit Card: Mastercard, VISA, Discover (circle one)
No.#_____ Exp. date _____

Make check or money orders payable to:
Yvette Jones
Virtuous Creations
P. O. Box 15868
Fort Wayne, IN 46885